LABORERS TOGETHER

Defining and Developing Your Relationship

with Your Pastor

JERRY FERRSO

First published in 2013 by Striving Together Publications, a ministry of Lancaster Baptist Church, Lancaster, CA 93535. Striving Together Publications is committed to providing tried, trusted, and proven resources that will further equip local churches to carry out the Great Commission. Your comments and suggestions are valued.

Striving Together Publications
4020 E. Lancaster Blvd.
Lancaster, CA 93535
800.201.7748
www.strivingtogether.com

Cover design by Craig Parker
Layout by Craig Parker
Edited by Rob Byers and Danielle Mordh
Special thanks to our proofreaders

The author and publication team have put forth every effort to give proper credit to quotes and thoughts that are not original with the author. It is not our intent to claim originality with any quote or thought that could not readily be tied to an original source.

ISBN 978-1-59894-233-0
Printed in the United States of America

Contents

Introduction

Few people expected the outbreak of the Korean War. Just five years had passed since the end of World War II, and the two atomic bombs dropped on Japan in the final days of the war had sparked an intense nuclear arms race. No one wanted to see nuclear powers face off in another war, yet despite the desire of a weary world for peace, war broke out again. Korea had been divided into two sections following the Japanese surrender, and in May of 1950, the Communist North—backed by China and Russia—invaded the South.

General Douglas MacArthur, who was then in charge of the American forces occupying Japan, was placed in charge of the United Nations forces and tasked with defending South Korea. With characteristic brilliance, MacArthur managed the defense until reinforcements could arrive and then launched one of the most ambitious invasions in history with the Inchon landing. This turned the tide of the war in favor of South Korea. But when hundreds of thousands of Chinese "volunteers" poured across the border to join the fight, the balance of power shifted again.

By 1951, stability had been obtained on the battlefield, but Korea remained divided. MacArthur had publicly complained about the restraints placed on what he was allowed to do in fighting the war. Asked by a reporter if not being allowed to attack the Chinese forces along the Yalu River in North Korea was hindering his efforts, MacArthur replied that it was indeed "an enormous handicap, unprecedented in military history."

MacArthur's public expression of his disapproval of decisions being made in Washington infuriated

President Harry Truman. After consulting with the Joint Chiefs of Staff and the Secretary of Defense, Truman relieved MacArthur of his command. Truman later said, "I fired him because he wouldn't respect the authority of the President."

Military experts still debate the issue of whose approach to the war was better—MacArthur or Truman. The Korean War ended not in victory but in a stalemate that dragged on for years and left nearly sixty thousand American troops dead on the battlefield. It is possible that MacArthur's preferred tactic of more aggressive war would have changed that outcome, although we cannot know for certain. But there is no doubt that reinforcing the principle of civilian control of the military was vital to the kind of country we want America to be. Douglas MacArthur was a great leader and one of our most brilliant military minds, but his refusal to submit to authority prematurely ended his career.

The question of authority is one humanity has struggled with since the Fall of man. Throughout Scripture and history, men and women—even believers—have struggled with submitting to those God has placed in authority over them. God has designed and instituted authority, and He commands us to be in obedience to those in authority over us.

> *Let every soul be subject unto the higher powers. For there is no power but of God: the powers that be are ordained of God. Whosoever therefore resisteth the power, resisteth the ordinance of God: and they that resist shall receive to themselves damnation. For rulers are not a terror to good works, but to the evil. Wilt thou then not be afraid of the power? do that which is good, and thou shalt have praise of the same: For he is the minister of God to thee for good. But if thou do that which is evil, be afraid; for he beareth not the sword in vain: for he is the minister of God, a revenger to execute wrath upon him that doeth evil. Wherefore ye must needs be subject, not only for wrath, but also for conscience sake.*—ROMANS 13:1–5

Yet if we're honest, we would have to admit that we sometimes struggle with submission to authority. It goes against the grain of our culture which glorifies rebellion. It also goes against the grain of our proud and sinful nature which leads us to want to do things our own way. America has become the nation of "I did it my way." However, God expects us to set aside our pride and desire for control and obey the authorities He has placed in our lives.

At every level of society, God has placed people in authority. This is true in the home, in the school, in government, and in the church. In fact, most of us fill one or more roles of authority in addition to being under other authorities. It is important that we recognize the role of God in establishing each of these authorities. He has placed them in our lives according to His plan and purpose, and He commands us to obey them.

We begin our lives as children in submission to the authority of our parents. Are parents perfect? Mine weren't. (But then I haven't been a perfect parent either!) Even though parents are fallible and make mistakes, they are still an authority that God has ordained. They must be obeyed. God does not command children to obey their parents because the parents are always right but because children need an authority in their lives.

As we get older, we come under the authority of teachers. If you're like me, you still get nervous when you remember your high school English teachers! Trying to diagram sentences and learn the rules of grammar took a toll on me. Yet, when the teacher says, "Turn in your homework" or "Open your book to page 255," she expects to be obeyed because of the authority of her position. A teacher doesn't walk up to random people on the street and give them assignments and instructions. That is a function of her role as an authority figure in the classroom.

Many of us played sports and came under the authority of a coach. Maybe you remember running laps or doing wind sprints until you thought you were going to die. Coaches yell at the players and make them run drills over and over again until they get it right. Imagine trying that on some stranger on the street—it wouldn't go over very well. But when the coach blows the whistle, the authority of his position makes the players jump to do what he says.

When we take our vehicles on the road, we fall into another sphere of authority. If a policeman pulls up behind you with his lights on, you pull your car over to the side of the road and stop. If he asks for your license, registration, and proof of insurance, you hand them over. If a stranger asked you for that personal information, you wouldn't willingly give it up. But because of the authority of the policeman's position, you respond to his direction.

At work, we do whatever task the boss assigns. There is a word for people who insist on doing things their own way on the job—unemployed. Even if we do not like what we are instructed to do, the fact the boss has a position of authority dictates our response. Because we want to keep getting a paycheck, we carry out the assignments and instructions we are given.

We need authorities in our lives. And God commands that we submit to their leadership. These authorities are for our blessing. They keep things functioning smoothly. They are important to the way every part of society operates.

This is just as true in the church as it is anywhere. God has placed pastors to lead local congregations. While the role of a pastor is different than that of a teacher, coach, or police officer, it's still important that we recognize this position as part of God's plan. In fact, the Bible describes pastors as a gift from God for His people! God "gave...pastors and teachers; For the perfecting of the saints, for the work of the ministry, for the edifying of the body of Christ" (Ephesians 4:11–12). As pastors teach and preach God's Word, God uses them in this role to lead people to spiritual maturity, to equip them for serving Him, and to encourage and build up the church family.

In God's plan, the relationship between the pastor and church members becomes a divine partnership— the pastor providing leadership and church members responding. As we laborer together, God's work is accomplished, and God is glorified.

In these pages, let's explore the roles of our partnership in the church. First, we'll look at the responsibilities of the pastor, and then we'll see God's instructions for following the pastor's leadership.

Chapter One
The Role of the Pastor

For this cause left I thee in Crete, that thou shouldest set in order the things that are wanting, and ordain elders in every city, as I had appointed thee: If any be blameless, the husband of one wife, having faithful children not accused of riot or unruly. For a bishop must be blameless, as the steward of God; not selfwilled, not soon angry, not given to wine, no striker, not given to filthy lucre; But a lover of hospitality, a lover of good men, sober, just, holy, temperate; Holding fast the faithful word as he hath been taught, that he may be able by

1

sound doctrine both to exhort and to convince the
*gainsayers.—*Titus 1:5–9

There are many models for leadership in various church groups and denominations. Some churches are run from the top down by a large hierarchical organization like the Catholic church. Others are run from within by a group of people like a board of deacons or elders. But as we will see, the Bible pattern for the local New Testament church is that it is under the headship of Christ.

And he is the head of the body, the church: who
is the beginning, the firstborn from the dead;
that in all things he might have the preeminence.
—Colossians 1:18

The church belongs to Christ, and He is to have preeminence and worship. This truth should, of course, be practiced in our church worship. And it should be reflected in the leadership structure.

Although some denominations practice ecclesiastical hierarchy in church government, biblical churches recognize that the local church is under the direct authority of Christ. And who will answer to Christ for the leadership of the church? The pastor.

> *Obey them that have the rule over you, and submit yourselves:* ***for they watch for your souls, as they that must give account, that they may do it with joy, and not with grief: for that is unprofitable for you.***—HEBREWS 13:17

The biblical teaching regarding the God-given authority of the pastor is not always popular, but it is vital. Without leadership, the local church would not fulfill that which Christ has assigned her to do. Furthermore, without spiritual leadership, we would lose focus in our spiritual growth.

> *Remember them which have the rule over you, who have spoken unto you the word of God: whose faith follow, considering the end of their conversation.*
> —HEBREWS 13:7

The Greek word translated *rule* is *hegeomai*, which is the word for a strong leader—a prince, a governor or a chief. It indicates a position of leadership.

By heeding and following the biblical instruction we receive from our pastor, we place ourselves in a position to receive the blessings of obedience that God promises to those who obey His Word.

What does the Bible mean when it tells us to "remember" the pastor? It is talking about calling something to mind—in other words, acknowledging the position in which God has placed him and choosing to submit ourselves to God's plan for structure within the church.

No pastor is perfect, but if you have a pastor who is blameless, who lives according to God's Word, and who lovingly, graciously, and faithfully communicates God's Word to the church family, you should recognize that gift and be thankful for it!

I am thankful that God placed Paul Chappell as the pastor of my church, Lancaster Baptist Church. He has the God-given and sacred task of leading our church and its people. There is no doubt in my mind that God called him to that position, and I am thankful for it. I have personally benefited from his preaching ministry, from his example, and through his vision and faith. My family has benefited greatly from following his leadership. My four children were saved at Lancaster Baptist Church, and three of them have been married here.

To further understand and appreciate your pastor's role as God designed it, let's look at the five different words used in the New Testament for pastors. Each of these words gives us insight into the important duties that the pastor is expected by God to fulfill.

Elder—The Greek word translated *elder* is *presbyteros.* The idea is one who presides over an assembly. The term *elder* indicates to us that God expects the pastor of the church to give direction and leadership under the direction of God's Word and the leading of the Holy Spirit. Pastoral authority is not exercised in a vacuum. It is not just the pastor imposing his personal likes and dislikes on the church. Rather, it is the pastor leading as God directs and giving the people insight and instruction from the Bible so that they can follow God's plan for their lives.

Let the elders that rule well be counted worthy of double honour, especially they who labour in the word and doctrine.—1 TIMOTHY 5:17

The elders which are among you I exhort, who am also an elder, and a witness of the sufferings of Christ, and also a partaker of the glory that shall be revealed:—1 PETER 5:1

When the Constitutional Convention was held in Philadelphia in 1787, George Washington was the unanimous choice to preside over the group. The hero of the Revolutionary War, Washington was deeply respected by the men who gathered to shape the form of the government for the new nation. Though he spoke little during the public debates, his wisdom and influence were a guide for the structure of a government designed to ensure freedom for the people. In that secular setting, Washington played a role much like what the Bible word "elder" describes for the pastor.

Bishop—The Greek word translated *bishop* is *episkopos*. This word carries the idea of being an overseer—one who is responsible for workers. God's plan is not for the pastor to be the only worker in the church. God's design is for the pastor to equip, train, and lead the people of the church to do the work of God. As a bishop, the pastor oversees that work.

> *And he gave...pastors and teachers; For the perfecting of the saints, for the work of the ministry, for the edifying of the body of Christ:*
> —EPHESIANS 4:11–12

> *For a bishop must be blameless, as the steward of God; not selfwilled, not soon angry, not given to wine, no striker, not given to filthy lucre;*
> —TITUS 1:7

> *This is a true saying, If a man desire the office of a bishop, he desireth a good work. A bishop then must be blameless, the husband of one wife, vigilant, sober, of good behaviour, given to hospitality, apt to teach;*—1 TIMOTHY 3:1–2

If you've ever seen a big construction crew working on a major project, it usually looks like complete chaos. There are people running all kinds of equipment and working in multiple directions and tasks all at the same time. But if you watch for a little while, you'll notice an overseer. He will be giving instructions and directives to the different workers so that they are all working together to accomplish the design according to the blueprint. That is what the bishop is to do in the church.

A godly pastor will follow the blueprint given in Scripture. As a wise overseer, he will look at the big picture and direct his co-laborers to build their lives on the principles of God's Word. If God has blessed you with a loving overseer, be thankful for his leadership in your life and church!

Shepherd—The Bible often refers to God's people as sheep. Admittedly, sheep are not impressive animals. We might wish that God had used powerful lions or majestic eagles or swift horses to describe us, but He knows us too well! Sheep are not the brightest of animals—they continually need someone to care for them and keep them safe.

First, the Lord Himself is our Shepherd. Psalm 23 assures us of His continual care for us. As our

Shepherd, He has ordained pastors as undershepherds to provide watch care.

> *Feed the flock of God which is among you, taking the oversight thereof, not by constraint but willingly; not for filthy lucre, but of a ready mind; Neither as being lords over God's heritage, but being ensamples to the flock. And when the chief Shepherd shall appear, ye shall receive a crown of glory that fadeth not away.*—1 PETER 5:2–4

We need undershepherds in the church—pastors who follow the Chief Shepherd and share His love and burden for God's people.

Shepherds feed the flock. Here we see a pastor's responsibility to provide spiritual nourishment as he preaches and teaches the Word of God.

Shepherds also warn and protect the flock from predators. We have an adversary dedicated to our destruction.

> *Be sober, be vigilant; because your adversary the devil, as a roaring lion, walketh about, seeking whom he may devour:*—1 PETER 5:8

Pastors are assigned and ordained by God as shepherds to protect the members of the church. Paul warned the leaders of the church at Ephesus, "For I know this, that after my departing shall grievous wolves enter in among you, not sparing the flock" (Acts 20:29). Pastors are to remain vigilant to doctrinal error that may be spread in the church.

One of the tenderest descriptions of the pastor's role is this word *shepherd.* Jesus Christ is the Chief Shepherd, and under His authority the pastor takes the responsibility for feeding and protecting the flock.

Preacher—The Greek word translated *preacher* is *keryx.* This word describes a herald who brings official messages from the king to the people. He does not speak his own opinions or by his own authority, but he does speak with great authority, for he is representing someone who has power and the right to command.

What a gift to have a God-given messenger proclaiming truths given from the King of kings!

In William Shakespeare's classic historical play *Henry V*, a French herald named Montjoy comes before Henry V and the following conversation takes place:

The king asks, "What shall I know of thee?"

Montjoy replies, "My master's mind."

Henry commands, "Unfold it."

Montjoy says, "Thus says my king" and proceeds to lay out the demands of the French monarch.

Montjoy was not there to express his own opinion but to deliver the message of the king. That is what a godly, Christ-centered pastor does when he preaches— he delivers, not preferences and opinions, but the message of our Lord to the people of the church.

Some of the strongest instructions to pastors in the New Testament relate to this responsibility to preach God's Word.

> *I charge thee therefore before God, and the Lord Jesus Christ, who shall judge the quick and the dead at his appearing and his kingdom; Preach the word; be instant in season, out of season; reprove, rebuke, exhort with all longsuffering and doctrine.*
> —2 TIMOTHY 4:1–2

Whom we preach, warning every man, and teaching every man in all wisdom; that we may present every man perfect in Christ Jesus.
—COLOSSIANS 1:28

My pastor is a well-educated man, but the power of his message is not his learning. Some powerful preachers over the years have been less educated. The authority of a preacher's message comes from its source. If a man simply preaches opinions and popular psychology, he has no authority in his message. But if a pastor preaches from the Word of God, he can speak with authority.

Over the years, I have seen my pastor pour out his heart as he labors in the Word—studying, preparing, and preaching—so our church family will not be tossed about by the winds of change and culture but instead will be rooted and grounded and built up in Christ. Every week he courageously declares the whole counsel of God. And, the people of the church need that. I need that. And I am thankful for it.

When your pastor preaches God's Word, heed it. And understand that you are receiving a vitally important message on behalf of God Almighty.

Teacher—The Greek word translated *teacher* is *didaskalos.* The idea is one who is fitted and prepared to give instruction to others. Every good pastor is first a student of the Word of God so that he is able to impart to the members of the congregation what he has himself learned. God expects the pastor to be an instructor of the truths of Scripture to the people of the church.

> *Or ministry, let us wait on our ministering: or he that teacheth, on teaching;*—ROMANS 12:7

> *And he gave some, apostles; and some, prophets; and some, evangelists; and some, pastors and teachers; For the perfecting of the saints, for the work of the ministry, for the edifying of the body of Christ:*—EPHESIANS 4:11–12

When Alexander the Great was a young boy, his father, Philip of Macedon arranged for him to be taught by Aristotle. Aristotle was one of the leading thinkers of the day, and Philip realized that his son would need to be grounded in knowledge to prepare him to rule an empire. The impact of Aristotle's influence on Alexander was enormous. In the same way, many of us have benefited greatly from having good teachers.

When we walk into church for a service, we should come with anticipation, expecting to learn. I've been going to church for a long time, but I still learn new insights from the pulpit as I listen with open ears and an open heart to the pastor teach. We should be ready and eager to receive instruction from the man God has given to teach His Word.

Studying the different roles a pastor fills helps us understand the gift that has been given to us by God. When a pastor lives a blameless life, labors in the Word, leads people according to these principles laid out in Scripture, we benefit. Our families benefit. And our lives are changed. That is a treasure!

Chapter Two
Partnership with Your Pastor

Therefore, my brethren dearly beloved and longed for, my joy and crown, so stand fast in the Lord, my dearly beloved. I beseech Euodias, and beseech Syntyche, that they be of the same mind in the Lord. And I intreat thee also, true yokefellow, help those women which laboured with me in the gospel, with Clement also, and with other my fellowlabourers, whose names are in the book of life.

—PHILIPPIANS 4:1–3

Now that we've established the responsibilities of the pastor, what are our roles in the context of this relationship? Can we sit back and watch the pastor do the work of the ministry alone? Of course not! God's plan requires our active involvement.

Paul described members of the church at Philippi as his "fellowlabourers." This is translated from the Greek word *synergos*—from which we get our word *synergy*. The idea is that by working together we accomplish more than we could by working separately.

Some pastors are tired and worn out by the stress and pressure of having to carry the entire load of the work of the church. That is not God's design. He wants the members of the church to be in active partnership with the pastor, doing their part to bear the yoke and carry the weight. Every member of the church is expected to partner with the pastor so that the work of the Lord is not hindered.

Hebrews 13:7 not only tells us to remember those who have rule over us, but then it says, "whose faith follow." We are not meant to just sit and listen to the truth but instead to get up and walk in the truth just as the pastor is walking in the truth. The Greek word for *follow* is *mimeomai.* Those of us old enough to remember the days before laser printers and ink jets when we had to use mimeograph machines recognize that word—it means to imitate or copy. There are two parts to this process in God's design.

First, the pastor imparts Bible truth to the hearers. Hebrews 13:7 says pastors "have spoken unto you the word of God." Every time a pastor stands behind the sacred desk to preach or teach, he is charged by Almighty God to deliver the truths of the Word of God. We already looked at Paul's directive to Timothy, but it is worth examining again in this context.

> *I charge thee therefore before God, and the Lord Jesus Christ, who shall judge the quick and the dead at his appearing and his kingdom; Preach the word; be instant in season, out of season; reprove, rebuke, exhort with all longsuffering and doctrine.*
> —2 TIMOTHY 4:1–2

God holds pastors to a high standard. Those who are not faithful to preach the Word receive great judgment at His hand. Look at this warning from the Old Testament to prophets who do not faithfully declare the words of God:

Thus saith the LORD of hosts, Hearken not unto
the words of the prophets that prophesy unto you:
they make you vain: they speak a vision of their
own heart, and not out of the mouth of the LORD.
They say still unto them that despise me, The LORD
hath said, Ye shall have peace; and they say unto
every one that walketh after the imagination of his
own heart, No evil shall come upon you. For who
hath stood in the counsel of the LORD, and hath
perceived and heard his word? who hath marked
his word, and heard it? Behold, a whirlwind of
the LORD is gone forth in fury, even a grievous
whirlwind: it shall fall grievously upon the head of
the wicked.—JEREMIAH 23:16–19

When a faithful pastor preaches the Word of God,
his message is profitable for the church. In fact, his
message has many facets in its benefits.

All scripture is given by inspiration of God, and is
profitable for doctrine, for reproof, for correction,
for instruction in righteousness:—2 TIMOTHY 3:16

This verse teaches us that Scripture came from
the breath of God. As Paul was writing these words

they were not his ideas but God's. The Holy Spirit of God moved on Paul's heart and mind so that he wrote exactly the words God wanted us to read. There are four specific areas where we need to hear from God.

Doctrine—The word *doctrine* means teaching, a set of beliefs. The Bible is profitable for telling us what is right. We live in a world filled with deception and falsehood. Satan is constantly at work trying to convince us to believe his lies. We need to know what is true and certain—and the pastor gives us sound doctrine from the Bible.

Reproof—This is telling us what is wrong. Many times we continue to do wrong because we have been deceived into thinking that it is right. We need a pastor who will draw clear lines of distinction from Scripture. The courage to call sin by its real name is greatly needed in our day.

Correction—This is telling us how to take things that are wrong and make them right. It is not enough to only identify the error. There must also be guidance and loving instruction so that we can make the necessary corrections to get back on the right path.

God never commands us to do something without also providing the means by which we can do it.

Instruction in righteousness—This is telling us how to keep doing right. God does not want us to merely start out on the right path. He wants us to continue on it and remain faithful to the end. We need encouragement and reminders along the way to ensure that we continue to walk righteously.

After the pastor imparts Bible truth, we are to imitate it. "Whose faith follow" is the process where we duplicate what we have seen and heard from the pastor. Christianity is not a mental religion but an active one.

I love this statement by Warren Wiersbe: "Faith is not some kind of nebulous feeling that we work up; faith is confidence that God's Word is true, and conviction that acting upon that Word will bring His blessing." As the pastor teaches the Word, God does not want us to simply be *informed*. He wants us to be *transformed*. If we do not put into practice what we are hearing, we will not benefit from the message—no matter how good the message is.

But be ye doers of the word, and not hearers only, deceiving your own selves. For if any be a hearer of the word, and not a doer, he is like unto a man beholding his natural face in a glass: For he beholdeth himself, and goeth his way, and straightway forgetteth what manner of man he was. But whoso looketh into the perfect law of liberty, and continueth therein, he being not a forgetful hearer, but a doer of the work, this man shall be blessed in his deed.—JAMES 1:22–25

Not very many of us leave the house without a quick look in the mirror to make sure we look okay. When we look into the mirror of the Word of God, it is brutally honest with us. It never tells us we're doing right when we're doing wrong. It gives us a clear, unvarnished, honest answer as to whether our behavior is acceptable in the eyes of a holy God. But that is not enough to produce change. Seeing where we fall short as we look into the Word only identifies the problem. We need to take the next step and take action to fix the problem.

You can spend the rest of your life in faithful attendance at every service in a wonderful church with a gifted and godly pastor who regularly proclaims the truth of God's Word with boldness and the power of the Holy Spirit, but it will not do you any good unless you are putting the truth you hear into practice in your life. Just as you would starve to death sitting in a five-star restaurant and only smelling but never eating the food, your soul will starve unless you take the truths that are preached into your heart and put them into practice.

If we are living as God intends, our conduct will be fueled, guided, shaped, and directed by the truths we receive from the Word of God. While we have a responsibility to be individual students of the Bible on our own, we also need to receive biblical instruction and put it into practice in our lives.

Chapter Three
Cultivating Spiritual Responsiveness

Remember them which have the rule over you, who have spoken unto you the word of God: whose faith follow, considering the end of their conversation.
—HEBREWS 13:7

Just as may be the case in any role an authority may fill, the direction a pastor provides does us little good if we are not responsive to his leadership. This is why God instructs us to follow the pastor as he follows the Lord.

It falls on us to be willing to humble ourselves and follow God's structure for order in the church.

The original meaning of the word *humble* was to
"kneel down" or to "make low." We see a wonderful
illustration of humility in the upper room. Just a few
hours before His crucifixion, Jesus was celebrating the
Passover with His disciples. You may already know this
story, but take a moment to read it again. Sometimes
we miss the point.

> *Jesus knowing that the Father had given all things*
> *into his hands, and that he was come from God,*
> *and went to God; He riseth from supper, and laid*
> *aside his garments; and took a towel, and girded*
> *himself. After that he poureth water into a bason,*
> *and began to wash the disciples' feet, and to wipe*
> *them with the towel wherewith he was girded.*
> —JOHN 13:3–5

Walking along dusty roads left the feet very dirty,
and it was customary for the host or homeowner to
have a servant wash the feet of his guests. It was a
dirty and disgusting job. In fact, it was considered
so demeaning that a Hebrew slave could not be
commanded to do it. You could order a foreign slave

to wash feet, but to get a Hebrew slave to do it, the owner had to ask instead of command.

Yet Jesus Christ, the Lord of Heaven and earth, laid aside His outer garments, wrapped Himself in a towel, and knelt down to wash the feet of His disciples. These were men who just a few hours before had been arguing over which of them was the greatest. Among their number was Judas Iscariot, who in just a few hours would betray Jesus for thirty pieces of silver. Yet despite their pride and sinfulness, Jesus still washed their feet.

He did this not because they deserved it or merited it but because He was demonstrating a vital spiritual truth—the need for humility and submission.

If you walked into church and saw Jesus standing in the pulpit, you would certainly listen and want to do whatever He said. But what if it were instead your pastor—a man instructed by God to proclaim His Word? Would you listen to him and submit to the teaching of Scripture just as you would if Jesus were there?

There are two vital elements we must possess if we are to cultivate a right response to the biblical teaching and instruction of our pastor.

First, we must be spiritual. Submission does not come naturally to any of us. But when the Holy Spirit is in control of our lives, we find that we are able to yield to authority without rebellion.

> *But the fruit of the Spirit is love, joy, peace, longsuffering, gentleness, goodness, faith, Meekness, temperance: against such there is no law.*
> —Galatians 5:22–23

Those who are longsuffering, gentle, and meek do not find it hard to submit.

Ever since the Fall in the Garden of Eden, man has wanted to go his own way.

> *All we like sheep have gone astray; we have turned every one to his own way…*—Isaiah 53:6

Our natural tendency (even after we are saved) is to respond to instruction and correction by saying, "Nobody is going to tell me what to do." The only hope of submitting to pastoral authority—or any other authority for that matter—in a godly way is to do it in the power of the Holy Spirit.

> *For they that are after the flesh do mind the things of the flesh; but they that are after the Spirit the things of the Spirit. For to be carnally minded is death; but to be spiritually minded is life and peace…So then they that are in the flesh cannot please God.*—ROMANS 8:5–6, 8

Don't miss this truth. The "do it my way" attitude—what the Bible calls a carnal mind—leads to death. If we viewed submission as the life or death issue that it really is, we would find it easier to do what is right.

When we are spiritually minded and when we submit our will to God and to the leadership He has placed in our lives, we receive life and peace. That is truly what all of us want. We want life to go well. We want to be blessed. We want things to turn out well for our marriages and for our children. What God is telling us here is that we need to walk in the Spirit to experience that blessing.

Second, we must be surrendered. Jesus was the Son of God and Lord of Heaven and earth. He had rights—but He laid them aside to do the will of His Father.

> *Jesus saith unto them, My meat is to do the will of him that sent me, and to finish his work.* —JOHN 4:34

> *But I have greater witness than that of John: for the works which the Father hath given me to finish, the same works that I do, bear witness of me, that the Father hath sent me.*—JOHN 5:36

Understand what Jesus is saying here. Instead of doing His own thing, He did exactly what God sent Him to do. As a result, His life was a success. Can we say that about our lives? Are we surrendered to do exactly what God wants, no matter what that may be?

> *I beseech you therefore, brethren, by the mercies of God, that ye present your bodies a living sacrifice,*

holy, acceptable unto God, which is your reasonable service.—ROMANS 12:1

God's will and God's way are better than my way, and by surrendering to His will, I find it easier to properly respond to my pastor's leadership.

Leadership is essential in the church, and God has appointed the pastor to provide it. Beware of the prideful tendency of consistently pushing against the pastor's leadership.

Those who follow sports understand the need for players to submit to the coach. I read once that Roger Staubach, the quarterback who led the Dallas Cowboys to the World Championship in 1971, admitted it was difficult for him to not get to call his own signals. Coach Landry sent in every play. He told Staubach when to pass and when to run. Only in emergency situations could Staubach change the play. (And if he were to be so brazen, he had better be right!) Even though Staubach considered Coach Landry to have a "genius mind" when it came to football strategy, Staubach's pride said that he should be able to run his own team.

Staubach later said, "I faced up to the issue of obedience. Once I learned to obey, there was harmony, fulfillment, and victory."

In the church, God desires that we serve as co-laborers for Him. But He has appointed the pastor as the leader. Until we, like Staubach, face up to the issue of authority, we will constantly be frustrated. But when we submit to God's plan, we will experience the momentum of teamwork.

In our next chapter, let's examine how we can cooperate with the pastor's leadership with a good attitude and a joyful spirit.

Chapter Four
Your Attitude Toward Your Pastor

Obey them that have the rule over you, and submit yourselves: for they watch for your souls, as they that must give account, that they may do it with joy, and not with grief: for that is unprofitable for you.—HEBREWS 13:17

I heard this story from Pastor Chappell, and I love it. Every day, an old man sat in his rocking chair with his granddaughter outside a gas station, greeting tourists who passed through their town. One day, a man who seemed to be looking for somewhere to live asked, "So what sort of town is this?"

"What sort of town do you come from?" the old man replied.

The tourist answered, "Everyone criticizes everyone. It's really bad."

"That's just the way it is here," said the old man.

A few days later, another man asked, "So what sort of town is this?"

"What sort of town do you come from?" the old man replied again.

The tourist answered, "It's great. Everyone gets along so well."

"That's just the way it is here," said the old man.

After the second man left, the granddaughter said, "How come you told the first guy this was a bad place to live and the second guy this is a great place to live?"

"Because wherever you go, you take your attitude with you, and that's what makes it good or bad."

Our attitude toward our pastor is vitally important because to a large measure it determines how we view everything about the relationship. If we view the man God has placed in authority over our church through the lens of Scripture, it changes the way we feel about everything he does. God tells us that this man has an awesome responsibility— one day your pastor will answer to God for the spiritual condition of you and your family. That is a huge responsibility!

Realize this, the Bible says that it is profitable for you to submit to your pastor with a good attitude. Yes, it does make the pastor's job easier if you and the rest of the church members are not having to be repeatedly convinced to follow God's instruction. But that is not the reason God tells you to obey—it is for *your* sake, not the pastor's.

Obedience and submission promote your own spiritual health. Both strengthen your family and protect you against the wolves and lions that threaten you and your children. They make your church a more joyful and pleasant place to worship and serve. There is great profit in doing things God's way when it comes to your attitude toward your pastor.

When God gives your pastor a vision, get on board wholeheartedly. Don't critique and nit-pick and look for flaws in his plan. Find out how you can help and join hands with him in the work. Put your talents and spiritual gifts to work to help the pastor accomplish his God-given vision, and you will profit from it. (I'm not talking about getting your name in the church paper or being recognized. I'm referring to the profit of God's approval and hearing Him say, "Well done.")

I love the biblical story of Jonathan fighting against the Philistines. The Israelites were outnumbered, and the Philistines had much better weapons. From a human standpoint, there was no way for Israel to win. But Jonathan had faith in God. He went out one day and saw a garrison of the Philistines. He said to his armor-bearer, "Let's go over there and see if God will help us teach them a lesson." That's a great demonstration of faith and vision in action, but look what his armor-bearer said in response.

> *And his armourbearer said unto him, Do all that is in thine heart: turn thee; behold, I am with thee according to thy heart.*—1 SAMUEL 14:7

What a great attitude!

The next time your pastor announces a project, take him aside and say, "If you want to charge that hill, I'm going to charge it with you. My heart is committed to helping you do all that God put in your heart." Be sure you have him sit down first—you don't want him to fall over in shock! Seriously, there is no telling how much encouragement and help it would be to your pastor if he knew that you were standing with him and supporting him—ready to go to battle to help accomplish the vision God has placed on his heart. Join in with a positive attitude, and there's no limit to what can be done.

Our attitude toward our pastor should not only be positive, but we should also always maintain a prayerful attitude toward the man of God.

> Pray for us: for we trust we have a good conscience, in all things willing to live honestly.
> —Hebrews 13:18

Over and over in the epistles, we see Paul asking people to pray for him. Why? Because as a preacher of the gospel of Jesus Christ, Paul needed prayer. Even though he was an apostle and a faithful witness, he knew he needed the prayers of God's people.

> *Withal praying also for us, that God would open unto us a door of utterance, to speak the mystery of Christ, for which I am also in bonds:* —Colossians 4:3

> *Brethren, pray for us.*—1 Thessalonians 5:25

> *Finally, brethren, pray for us, that the word of the Lord may have free course, and be glorified, even as it is with you:*—2 Thessalonians 3:1

In the early days of his ministry, D. L. Moody was doing everything he could for God, but as he later confessed, he was largely working in the power of the flesh rather than the power of the Holy Spirit. As he preached at the YMCA in Chicago, Moody noticed two older women who came to the meetings. Afterward they would come and tell him that they were praying for him to receive the power of God for his work. At first Moody was annoyed, but then coming under conviction, he asked to pray with them.

Not long after, Moody was preparing for a trip to London to preach when something happened that changed his life and ministry forever. He told the story this way: "One day, in the city of New York—oh, what a day!—I cannot describe it, I seldom refer to it; it is almost too sacred an experience to name.... I can only say that God revealed Himself to me, and I had such an experience of His love that I had to ask Him to stay His hand. I went to preaching again. The sermons were not different; I did not present any new truths, and yet hundreds were converted. I would not now be placed back where I was before that blessed experience if you should give me all the world—it would be small dust in the balance." That transformation began with two ladies praying for one of God's servants.

If you will faithfully and seriously pray for your pastor, you may change the entire future of your church. Your pastor needs your prayers. The devil is out to get him. His family is under attack. His children face unique challenges and problems. Your pastor needs wisdom. He needs the Holy Spirit's power. He needs physical strength. He needs to stay pure and devoted to God. He needs discernment. God gives these things in answer to prayer. Are you asking Him for them for your pastor? Pray for your pastor just as regularly and faithfully as you pray for your own family.

Do you have a godly, Christ-centered leader as your pastor? If so, thank God for that gift!

Commit to be a person who loves, believes, prays for, supports, helps, encourages, and strengthens the hands of your pastor. Commit to working together with him to accomplish God's purposes for your life and church.

> *Only let your conversation be as it becometh the gospel of Christ: that whether I come and see you, or else be absent, I may hear of your affairs, that ye stand fast in one spirit, with one mind striving together for the faith of the gospel;*
> —Philippians 1:27

Conclusion

For we are laborers together with God: ye are God's husbandry, ye are God's building.—Hebrews 13:7

I love the truth given by the Apostle Paul to the church of Corinth: "we are laborers together with God." While God calls the pastor to lead and the congregation to follow as he follows Christ, Paul emphasized the big picture—we are all serving God together.

God has gifted each member of the church family in a different way. Discover and understand your gifts and then use them to serve the Lord in the capacity He chooses. As we focus, not on what others are doing, but on how God has called us to serve within the local church, we further Christ's work in our lives and in the life of our churches.

One of the biggest ways to encourage your pastor is to commit to serve God with him. One of the greatest ways to reap blessings for your family is to sow seeds of service in the Lord's work. One of the proven ways to grow spiritually is to commit your work and labor to the Lord.

Remember the big picture: God has given the pastor and the people different roles, but He gives us all the same purpose of laboring together with Him. Commit to fulfilling this purpose and savor the benefits God gives as a result!

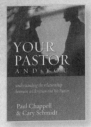
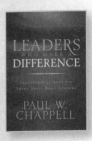
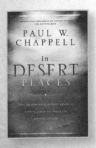

Visit us online

strivingtogether.com

wcbc.edu